FREEDOM

FROM

NATIONAL

DEBT

FREEDOM
FROM
NATIONAL
DEBT

FRANK N. NEWMAN

WHY U.S. TREASURY SECURITIES

- OFTEN CALLED "NATIONAL DEBT" – ARE IMPORTANT FORMS OF SAVINGS FOR MILLIONS OF INVESTORS

- ARE SAFER THAN MONEY

- ARE NOT LIKE PERSONAL DEBT FOR THE NATION AND ITS CITIZENS

- DO NOT HAVE TO BE "PAID OFF" BY TAXPAYERS

- CANNOT PRESENT THE PROBLEMS OF EUROZONE NATIONS

AND WHY AMERICA DOES NOT NEED TO FEAR "NATIONAL DEBT"

Two Harbors Press
212 3rd Avenue North, Suite 290
Minneapolis, MN 55401
612.455.2293
www.TwoHarborsPress.com

ISBN-13: 978-1-62652-038-7
LCCN: 2013903557

Distributed by Itasca Books

Cover Design by Kristeen Wegner
Typeset by James Arneson

Printed in the United States of America

TABLE *of* CONTENTS

Acknowledgments and Appreciation

Thanks to my wife, Liz, for her continuous support, encouragement, and thoughtful questions.

Thanks to good friends with strong but open minds who offered perceptive comments and suggestions.

Thanks especially for the valuable help from my son, Daniel Newman, who edited this book, and helped me work through some of the most challenging aspects of the logic and the implications. Many of the ideas in the book were developed by testing initial thoughts with him, drawing on his strong insights and broad range of knowledge. The analysis and exposition are sharper and more clear as a result of his help.

Introduction

America's worries about "national debt" have come to dominate national debate on a wide range of public policy issues. Discussions of national undertakings – including infrastructure repair, jobs programs, military modernization, disease prevention, and international strategy - have all been stifled because of this fear. America has convinced itself that it can no longer afford, as a nation, to do many of the productive things that it has done so well over its history.

That's a great shame, not just because America remains a nation of tremendous resources in every sense, but because the underlying assumptions about U.S. government financial instruments are not correct. America can never face the debt problems of nations like Greece, because it has a fundamentally different financial system.

This short book explains why such fears should not hold back America, and why even the expression "national debt" is neither meaningful nor appropriate for the United States.

The book asks some underlying questions: What does "national debt" really mean in the modern financial system of the U.S.? What harm has it actually done to America? Why have none of the frequent predictions about terrible consequences of U.S. Treasury issuance come true? Why do some countries, despite large amounts of government securities relative to GDP, have very strong government bond markets, while bonds of several eurozone countries face major challenges? The conventional views just do not provide coherent and convincing explanations. It's time to think in new ways about the underlying assumptions. The book explores these and other related issues, stepping back to think anew about the fundamentals.

In so doing, this book puts the expression "national debt" in quotation marks when referring to U.S. Treasuries, since they do not actually constitute debt in the sense commonly implied. The term "debt" carries connotations that are strongly challenged by the analysis here, and the quotation marks are intended to invite the reader to step back and look at the underlying issues.

Many people believe that the government has to borrow good, safe money from the public, and that someday we'll be taxed in order to repay the debt. But that established view does not properly reflect the modern U.S. financial system, in which *"national debt" is an expression for U.S. Treasury securities, issued in U.S. dollars.* The book addresses what "money" really is in a modern financial system, and how it relates to Treasuries, and then explains why America has no financial instruments that warrant the term national debt.

This is a critical issue for economic policy in America - and around the world. Misunderstanding of the modern nature of money and Treasuries (or their equivalents in other countries) needlessly confines thinking about economic approaches to reducing unemployment and growing GDP. *The reasons often alleged for fear of "national debt" are not valid for the U.S. and other nations with similar structures of financial systems.* There is a very different situation for the eurozone nations and other countries that raise funds in currencies that are not their own. Greece, Portugal, Ireland, and other nations that do not have their own currencies and financial systems *do* have obligations that should be considered national debt.

America can have freedom from fear of national debt by recognizing the real nature of the Treasury securities that are referred to by that expression, and their relationship to what is called money. The concerns are left over from an earlier time, when the U.S. financial system was very different.

Of course, the conclusions that the U.S. does not really have "national debt" in the usual sense of the expression, and that we should not worry about it or hold back economic programs out of fear of it, may seem radical to some, and the book tries to explain the logic carefully. It addresses a number of the common concerns, analyzing each one to explain why it is not really an issue to fear.

Once the alleged reasons for that fear have been demonstrated to be unfounded, then it becomes possible to move on to key policy issues, including high unemployment and slow growth, and to options such as infrastructure and defense maintenance and modernization, and tax reduction. This is not the only issue for the U.S. economy, of course, but is hugely important, and influences many other aspects of our economy, the lives of millions of people, and America's position in the world.

Freedom from these concerns does not mean that annual deficits should be ignored. The book explains why, in times of a cold, slow economy, with high unemployment, "heat" – deficits for economic support, through government spending programs such as infrastructure, and lower taxes – can help greatly. In times of a very hot economy, with low unemployment and high capacity utilization, "air conditioning" – reduction in the deficit – is appropriate. And, programs to control deficits ten years from now, when we hope the economy will be hot, are important. But none of these issues need be influenced by concern over the amount of Treasury securities outstanding.

This book uses some of the analysis developed in the author's recent book *Six Myths that Hold Back America - And What America Can Learn from the Growth of China's Economy ("Six Myths")*. That book challenges some basic concepts of current economic thinking, and reaches some unconventional conclusions from logic about the financial system, including:

- Saving cannot generate productive business Investment; it's the other way around: Investment generates economic Saving.

- Deficits do not reduce national Saving or Investment.
- Issuance of Treasury securities (deficit financing) cannot "use up" equivalent amounts of funds intended for private-sector use.

The theme of this book is *very* different from traditional views, but is based on a logical approach to looking at the financial system. *Six Myths* contains one quotation from John Maynard Keynes; it fits so well here that I'll repeat it before beginning the exposition and analysis:

"The difficulty lies, not in the new ideas, but in escaping from the old ones. . . ."

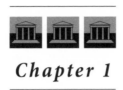

Chapter 1

What is Money?
The nature of money and Treasuries

In order to fully understand the nature of Treasury securities ("national debt"), we need first to focus on what money really is.

Many people think of money – in addition to being a medium of exchange to buy and sell things - as the "real thing" for a financial asset, the good, safe stuff. They think of the government as borrowing this good, reliable value from investors who need incentives to invest their "secure money" in Treasuries. And many people who have been lectured a thousand times about the "evils" of "national debt" believe that the U.S. government will have to generate enough money revenue, through future taxes, to "pay off" all the Treasury securities that have been issued to finance deficits.

But none of these beliefs are true.

Financial assets in the U.S. encompass a range of assets denominated in dollar terms. Sometimes, people use the term money in a broad, general sense, to refer to how wealthy someone might be ("he has lots of money"). In financial terminology, "wealth" is the term used for such broad purposes, and includes "financial assets," such as bank deposits and investments in Treasury securities and corporate bonds and stocks, as well as other types of assets owned, such as real estate.[1] For economic purposes, and as used in this book, what is called money is not the same as wealth; money is just one class of financial asset, while Treasuries are another form of financial asset.

The term money is actually used in various ways even in Finance and Economics. The Federal Reserve System publishes figures for total deposits in U.S. banks.[2] The Fed also computes "money supply" figures for "M1," which includes certain deposits and currency, and "M2," which includes M1 plus certain other deposits and money market fund accounts for individuals. "M3," which includes even more categories, is no longer published by the Fed, although some private economists publish estimates. Economists looking at U.S. money or the "money supply" often use figures which are updated by the Fed each week: total deposits in banks are currently about $9 trillion, while M2 is currently about $10 trillion. Paper currency, though included in M1, is used primarily for

---

1   The Fed reports total financial assets in the U.S in excess of $150 trillion, with total assets roughly $200 trillion.

2   US dollars cannot exist outside of the U.S., as explained in Chapter 1 of *Six Myths*. Reported USD figures in foreign banks just reflect those banks' deposits at U.S. bank members of the Federal Reserve System. Foreign bank deposits are not included by the Fed in M1 or M2.

convenience with relatively small transactions, and is not very relevant when looking at alternative investment vehicles, including Treasuries.

This book generally uses the term "money" in a commonly-used way: U.S. dollar deposits in U.S. banks: "money in the bank." A very key point is that, since banks face risks every day, money is subject to credit risk, liquidity risk, and interest-rate risk.

Book def

Treas.

The term "Treasuries" is used to refer to all forms of securities issued to public investors by the U.S. Treasury Department, including what the Treasury calls "bills," "notes," and "bonds."

We should also be sure to have a clear understanding of the difference between "deficits" and "national debt." A government deficit measures the amount by which outlays exceed revenues in a particular period, usually a year. Each deficit is financed by issuing Treasury securities. *"National debt" refers here to the amount of Treasuries outstanding and held by investors at any time, as a result of financing deficits over many years.*

Money is an instrument of value and, in some forms an instrument of exchange. Paper currency is issued and honored by the government, but most money is *created by banks*. A portion of money is readily usable in commerce to make payments, but some of it is not—savings accounts and term deposits, for example, need to be converted to another form (checking) before they can be used for payment purposes. Banks have deposits at the Fed ("reserves"), which are guaranteed by an arm of the U.S. government (the Fed), but most deposits at commercial banks have guarantees by the FDIC on only limited amounts. (Money-market funds, which are partially included in M2, have no guarantee.) In contrast, all Treasuries are fully guaranteed by "the full faith and credit" of the U.S. government, and play a unique and essential role in the financial/monetary system.

This book focuses on U.S. dollars, and when referring to investors, means investors who hold U.S. Dollar ("USD") assets and have to decide which financial assets to hold. The book does not try to address the questions facing a holder of international assets in various currencies, trying to decide which currency to invest in, as well as which kind of financial asset. For the U.S. financial system, it is U.S. dollars that matter; if any investor who holds USD assets decides to sell some in exchange for Yen or Pounds, then the seller of those currencies will then hold the USD assets, and will need to decide about the tradeoffs between risk, return, and liquidity for alternative USD assets.

1.1 Bank Money

Most of the money in the U.S. financial system was created by commercial banks, and is backed by the banks, not by the government; it is essentially "bank money." As the banking system makes new loans, it creates equal amounts of new deposits – "bank money"; this process is explained in Chapter 2. Many people mistakenly believe that investors offer "real, safe money" to the government when they invest in Treasuries, and need an incentive to do so. In fact, investors are actually allocating their financial assets between various types, including bank deposits, each with its own characteristics of risk and relative rates of return set by the market. Investors in specific maturing Treasury securities can have those government-guaranteed investments replaced by bank money, which is only partially guaranteed. In aggregate, as explained in Chapter 2, the full amount of Treasuries outstanding has never been and will never be replaced by bank money—the aggregate total will remain outstanding essentially permanently. Many investors have the principal of their maturing securities reinvested directly into new Treasuries, with no bank money changing hands.

1.2 Money is Never Consumed

Money is never "used up." Financial assets vary in *Can be reduced* market value, but the principal values of bank deposits and Treasuries are never consumed; they are just passed from one investor to another. When someone makes a purchase or investment for $100, the banking system simply records a change in ownership of that $100. Person A may feel his or her $100 is gone, but it has just been added to another account at a U.S. bank (member of the Federal Reserve System). For the U.S. banking system as a whole, the amount of money (bank deposits) remains unchanged. As explained further in Chapter 2, money is always *created* by banks as they make loans, and is sometimes created by the Fed. Similarly, the total money supply can be *reduced* in limited ways: by the Fed when it sells securities, or when securities that the Fed holds are paid down; by the banking system when total loans are declining, and the deposits created with the loans are extinguished; and by bank failures. But no actions of depositors or investors can reduce the money supply. Money is not a consumed good; it is constantly recycled.

Similarly, Treasury securities do not "use up" money. When the Treasury issues securities, it doesn't put the cash it receives in exchange under a big mattress in the basement of the Treasury building. Over time, the government distributes essentially the same amount that it raises through taxes and Treasury issuance, and the amount of money in the financial system is not changed by this process.

While government *spending* (direct and indirect) on goods and services could compete with private sector spending for real productive resources in a full-employment economy, spending cannot actually "use up" money in the financial system. In the unusual circumstance of a full-employment economy, additional government deficit spending would likely put inflationary pressure on the economy. That is a key reason why government deficits that are projected for a boom year 10 or 20 years in the future need to be addressed. But increases in Treasuries ("government debt") are extremely useful now, during a slow economy with high unemployment. Economic implications of using Treasuries to support the economy during slow times are discussed in Chapter 9.

Often investors think about such issues in terms of their own individual portfolios, rather than the system as a whole. "If I had been reserving some funds in my portfolio for new investments, and I have just now used $100,000 of that reserve to buy Treasuries, then the money is gone, and I cannot invest that $100,000 in a corporate bond." But while that is true for that one investor, it misses the picture for the overall financial system. (This is a form of the "Fallacy of Composition," discussed more fully in Chapter 3 of *Six Myths*.) Deficits, which are recorded in the National Income Accounts as "dis-Saving" by the government, always mean an equivalent increase in private sector Saving – in the form of Treasuries. As new Treasury buying opportunities are introduced just after the Treasury Department has paid new money into the system, both the new Treasuries and the cash distributed by the government find a happy balance: the cash placed into the system by government outlays finds an interest-bearing home in the newly-issued Treasuries.

A similar dynamic applies with the issuance of new corporate bonds, but of course without the government

Seem strange: investors had one asset (cash) + now they have a different asset: bond
Company has new asset, but also new liability

FRANK N. NEWMAN

guarantee. When a corporation issues bonds for $100 million, investors deliver bank money to the corporation, which then deposits the funds in its bank account. The corporation records new liabilities of $100 million for the bonds, and new assets of $100 million in the form of bank deposits. The total money supply (bank deposits) is unaffected – no money is "used up," but investors now own another $100 million of financial assets, so total financial assets in the USD system have increased. The individual corporate bonds are paid off at maturity, but corporations are often issuing new bonds, and the aggregate total outstanding can continue to increase. Since 2000, aggregate U.S. corporate bonds of nonfinancial companies have risen from about $3 trillion to about $5 trillion.

also have liability

This leads to another reason why it is important to look at total financial assets, not just one component such as what is defined as the money supply. For example, suppose that a corporation wants to borrow $100 million to buy some new equipment, and a group of consumers want to borrow another $100 million for personal consumption. If they both borrow the money from banks, then the money supply will increase by $200 million. If the corporation raises the money through a bond issuance, or from a commercial finance company, and the consumers borrow the money from consumer finance companies rather than banks, then the money supply will not show an increase. These transactions involve the creation of the same amount of total financial assets in the system, and the same amount of demand and spending, but one method happens to record an increase in the money supply and the other method does not.

1.3 Treasuries are safer than money

Treasuries are always safer than money (bank deposits). The recent crisis provides an especially sharp illustration of the power of that extra safety. In 2008 and 2009, concerns about the risks of bank deposits (money) grew strongly, as markets worried about the safety of many banks. Depositors feared bank credit risk (insolvency) and liquidity risk - the ability to withdraw their money in a timely manner. Some money-market funds with large deposits in banks, but no government guarantees, fell below par value and faced liquidity crises. Investors increasingly valued the safety of U.S. Treasury securities, and bid down yields on Treasuries. The U.S. government – the Treasury, the Fed, the FDIC - came to the rescue of the banking system, providing liquidity, capital, and guarantees, and thus rescued a large amount of money. Large amounts of deposits and even some bank bonds were guaranteed, backed by the U.S. Treasury. When the Treasury invested money into banks, in order to make them safer, that cash came from investors who bought new Treasury securities at a time when the investors were uneasy about the security of money (deposits) in major banks. Even the guarantee of the first $250,000 of deposits in a bank account is backed by the understanding that the government will use the proceeds from issuance of Treasuries as needed to fulfill that partial guarantee of bank deposits. Of course, there are many good and sound banks, but Treasuries are used to provide protection for the U.S. banking system, and are fundamentally safer than money, which is largely a form of liability of commercial banks.

One form of money that is as safe as Treasuries is paper currency, which is printed by the U.S. Treasury and distributed by the Fed, but comprises only about 10% of the money supply. The government guarantees the dollars embedded in each $20 bill. Both paper currency and Treasury securities have the full backing of the U.S. government.

Treasuries are critical tools in the balance of both the economic and financial systems. A very large portion of U.S. dollar financial assets is priced with interest rates based on the risk-free rates of U.S. Treasuries; there are very good reasons for that. Other U.S. dollar financial instruments are directly or indirectly dependent on the deep Treasury market. If a bank or company fails, the Treasury market continues on strongly. We saw that in 2008 and 2009 a range of financial and industrial companies were rescued by the U.S. government, using financing provided by issuance of Treasuries. But banks, securities firms, asset managers, and industrial companies own large amounts of Treasuries, directly or indirectly, through the banks, pension funds, and other investments, and have hundreds of thousands of financial transactions that utilize Treasuries. The finances of America are extensively intertwined with Treasury securities.

1.4 New ways of thinking about Treasuries in the financial system

We can now look at modern financial systems with a new perspective which applies to the United States of America, the UK, Japan, China, and many other nations which have their own currencies (not pegged to another), have their own central banks and banking and financial systems, and finance themselves in their own currencies. (The eurozone nations do not fit these criteria.)

The old thinking about the Treasury needing to "borrow" bank money from investors does not properly describe the modern financial system. Today, investors make considered decisions to allocate their financial assets in various ways, including in Treasury securities, given their perceptions of risk in the financial system and the banking system at the time. Treasuries today are much like time deposits directly with the U.S. Treasury, but better than similar deposits in commercial banks, since Treasuries are fully backed by the U.S. government, and tradable[3]. Treasuries provide especially safe and

---

3   An analogy between Treasuries and a government (Fed) bank has been used by Warren Mosler, in "Seven Deadly Innocent Frauds of Economic

highly liquid vehicles to keep funds invested over time or available for use soon. It is always rational for markets to set interest rates on U.S. Treasuries lower than for the comparable maturities of bank deposits. (In eurozone nations, as explained in Chapter 4, things can be very different.)[4] Corporate bond rates are typically set at spreads over Treasury rates, reflecting perceived risk measures. Longer maturity Treasury bonds do not have comparable bank term deposit rates, since banks do not typically offer term deposits beyond about 5 years. So rates on long bonds are set by the market based on various factors such as estimates of inflation in the future.

Once we recognize that U.S. Treasuries provide both a means of payment for the U.S. government and vehicles for investors to keep financial assets with a government guarantee, the concerns often stated about "borrowing" and "national debt" fall in a different light. Typically, depositors do not think of banks as "borrowing" from them. Banks and the Treasury provide two of many different ways for investors to hold their USD financial assets.

Policy." That book and *Six Myths* take different approaches to reach some similar conclusions. This author recommends Mr. Mosler's book, as well as various writings by academic proponents of "Modern Monetary Theory" or "Neo-Chartalism," including L. Randall Wray (The Levy Economics Institute of Bard College,), James K. Galbraith (University of Texas), Scott Fullwiler (Wartburg College), and Bill Mitchell (University of Newcastle, New South Wales, Australia).

4   Also, there are times when some banks, awash in liquidity, post very low rates for deposits, because they simply do not need more deposits and do not want to pay up for them.

A more modern way to think of the Treasury auction process is not as the U.S. government "borrowing" safe money from people. Rather, the auctions are ways to allocate, through a market process, a limited supply of new Treasury securities to bidders who want to invest in the safety and liquidity of Treasuries.

[handwritten margin note: ? buying # or selling bonds]

Treasuries play an extremely important role as financial instruments for investors to keep savings. The $9½ trillion of Treasuries in public hands are financial assets representing savings of pension funds, nonprofit charities, insurance companies, industrial companies, individuals, families, family trusts, government entities, universities, etc. That amounts to more than the total dollars held in all U.S. bank deposits combined.

[handwritten note: Doesn't this assume banks have unlimited ability to create credit (money)]

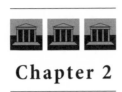

Chapter 2

How Money (bank deposits) and Treasuries are continually exchanged

B efore addressing some of the common misconceptions about "national debt," it will be helpful to
look at some background about how key aspects of the
insides of the financial system work.

2.1 How Deposits Grow

you can I savings but he is focused on one component only

There are often misunderstandings about how the total
amounts of deposits grow in an economy and a banking
system. Many commentators state or imply that somehow,
if we could get depositors to try to save more money,
then that would lead to increases in total deposits in the
system, and more money available for banks to lend. But
that is *not possible*, since deposits by every depositor have
to come from withdrawals from another bank account.
It is impossible for depositors to increase total deposits
in the nation, no matter how hard they might try. As
explained in Chapter 1, people do not "use up" money

when they spend: it just moves from one deposit account to another; similarly, when people save, it does not add to total deposits, since each person's income comes from another deposit account. The main source of growth of deposits in a nation comes from the banks, which *create* money as they make loans.

An individual bank may want to increase its market share of deposits, in order to improve its liquidity, because if some of its deposits are moved to another bank, then the first bank must provide cash (reserves) to cover that amount in its Fed account, as the Fed moves reserves from the account of the first bank to the account of the second bank. A bank that has increased its deposits may feel more confident about its liquidity position, but money just moves from one bank to another without changing the overall total of deposits. The banking system cannot actually use deposits of one customer to lend to another: it must create new deposits exactly equal to its new loans, and can increase total deposits only by making loans (or buying investments from the market). A bank making a loan needs to increase the deposit account of the borrower by the amount of the loan, but cannot erase from its books the liabilities it has to existing depositors. This process is illustrated in Appendix A.

The central bank, like the Fed in America, also has the ability to increase or decrease total deposits, although in the U.S., the amount of money created by the Fed is much smaller than the amount that the banks have created. The Treasury, as explained earlier, does make relatively small and temporary additions to total deposits, but that process is quickly balanced as the Treasury issues securities. When a bank or the Fed creates deposits, it increases the money supply, thus adding a particular kind of financial asset to the financial system. When the Treasury issues securities, it adds a different kind of financial asset to the system.

2.2 A Look at Aggregate Financial Investments in the Nation

It can be very helpful, in looking at some of these issues, to think of the entire financial system in aggregate – as if it were one integrated institution serving the nation's financial functions. The system marvelously balances itself every day - with help from the Fed, in its role as central bank, which provides flexibility for timing differences, frictions, etc. The Treasury and the Fed are both parts of the U.S. government; they have different responsibilities within the U.S. financial system, but often work together.

When the Treasury makes distributions, then replenishes its Fed account by issuing new securities (in addition, of course, to collecting taxes), then total financial assets increase, but there is no change in the money supply or in equity risk or credit risk in the financial system. This process is illustrated in Appendix B.

In the process of Treasury issuance and redemption, the money involved changes hands but cannot leave the U.S. financial system. There is a huge, deep market for Treasuries, with an average of over $500 billion *per day* traded. Typically when the Treasury issues securities, it has already distributed funds to the bank accounts of investors redeeming securities and to recipients of government payments, from the Treasury account at the Fed. Treasury has been generally keeping about $100 billion, sometimes up to $300 billion, on deposit at the Fed— that is in addition to the hundreds of billions of other assets, including gold and silver, held by the Treasury. Sometimes the Treasury issues securities temporarily in advance of disbursement, mostly as part of planning for seasonal variations. Generally, the Treasury uses bank money newly received from tax collection and Treasury issuance to replenish its deposit accounts at the Fed.

When the Treasury distributes funds, the nation's deposits are initially increased. Where can the bank money go? Let's look at an example, excluding the portion covered by taxes. Typically, before the Treasury issues $20 billion of securities, the government has distributed $20 billion to the public from its account at the Fed: redeeming maturing Treasuries, paying companies that provide goods and services for the government, for payments to individuals, etc. Many investors simply "roll over" their Treasury securities, replacing maturing ones with newly issued ones, and taking just the interest. For example, perhaps $10 billion of the $20 billion issue might be in that category. The Treasury pays out the other $10 billion to the private sector. At that point, a set of participants in the U.S. financial system will have the extra $10 billion in their bank accounts and will look to place those funds.

The money supply has been increased by $10 billion, and the new dollars move around within the overall US financial system. All the Treasuries previously available are already owned by investors, and prior auctions had demand that exceeded the amount offered. As the new Treasuries are auctioned, the demand is filled by exactly the $10 billion offered, and the money supply returns to its prior level. In the whole of the U.S. financial system, the only place to put the money is into the new Treasuries that are being auctioned—or otherwise just leave the funds in banks. If some investors choose to buy other financial assets with those new funds, such as corporate bonds or stocks, then someone else—the sellers of those assets—will end up with the bank deposits, and will be looking for a place to invest them. There are no other USD financial assets to invest in that are not already owned by someone. And the dollars cannot go to another country; an individual investor can choose to invest some dollars in assets in another country, but then the foreigners who sold those assets would just own the same dollars in U.S. banks. The aggregate of all investors have, in the end, two choices: leaving the extra $10 billion of cash in bank deposits, which earn very little, if any, interest, and are not guaranteed by the government beyond \$250,000[1]; or exchanging some of their bank money for the new Treasuries, which pay interest and have the "full faith and credit" of the United States.

For most people, of course, \$250,000 is a lot of money. But very large amounts of money, way in excess of that figure, are held by families, corporations, pension funds, money-market funds, mutual funds, foundations, etc. For the investors of hundreds of thousands of dollars, or millions, or hundreds of millions, \$250,000 is far too small for significant protection. Investors are willing to hold some amount of large financial assets in as deposits at what they believe to be the most sound banks, for convenience, and as long as banks offer sufficient interest rates to compensate for the additional risk compared to Treasuries. Markets very rationally go to Treasuries for maximum safety, investing in all the Treasuries that are available.

Banks could also buy some of the new Treasury securities, and would be especially likely to buy if the interest rates on Treasuries were just slightly higher. At the time of this writing, U.S. banks hold about \$1.4 trillion of excess reserves at the Fed, far beyond the amounts held prior to 2008. Currently, short-term Treasury bills are yielding less than 10 basis points (one tenth of one percent). The Fed has set the rate it pays on excess reserves left by banks

---

1   Except for a temporary unlimited guarantee for certain non-interest accounts, expiring at the end of 2012.

at the end of the day at 25 basis points (one quarter of one percent). The Fed could lower the rate it pays banks, creating more incentive for banks to seek other income; or rates on Treasuries might rise a little; then the banks would have a clear financial incentive to buy net new Treasuries. Some banks also invest in intermediate-term Treasuries with higher yields, thus taking some interest-rate risk, but no credit risk.

The U.S. banking system could actually purchase a *very* large amount of Treasuries. As banks buy Treasuries from investors, they create money in the accounts of the sellers, similar to the process of creating money when they make loans. Banks must transfer only a fraction of the new deposits from their excess reserve accounts at the Fed to their required reserve accounts. That amounts to a very small reduction in the current level of excess reserves. It takes only about $2 of the excess reserves in the banking system to buy $100 of Treasuries. Banks could keep buying Treasuries *far* beyond their current $1.4 trillion holdings of excess reserves. This process is illustrated in Appendix C.

2.3 Treasuries and the Fed

The Fed has a whole range of tools it can use to help the stability of the U.S. financial system. Some are unlikely to ever be needed. For example, if for some extraordinary reason investors and banks were slow to buy all the new Treasuries, and the Fed chose not to use its tools to make the Treasuries more attractive to banks, and if short-term Treasury rates did not rise above the Fed rate paid to banks on excess reserves, then the Fed could buy Treasury securities from the market, thus creating new deposits, with excess reserves, that could be reinvested in new Treasuries.

In essence, the money distributed by the Treasury from its account at the Fed returns to the Fed in one way or another. At first, that money goes into bank accounts and is placed by the banks into their excess reserve accounts at the Fed. When new Treasuries are issued, investors withdraw from their bank accounts to purchase the new securities, and the money sent to the Treasury moves into the Treasury account at the Fed - from where it started. If any money distributed by the Treasury were left in the banks, it would still be in the excess reserve accounts at the Fed.

2.4 Money, Treasuries, and inflation

We know that some commentators express great concerns about what they call Fed "monetization of debt" or "printing money." But experience should put those concerns in perspective. The main unease seems to be a concern that if the Fed buys Treasuries, it will increase the money supply and thus perhaps cause excessive growth in lending, thus excessive demand, higher interest rates, and inflation. But let's examine that concern.

In the U.S., the Fed has often bought Treasuries from the market as part of its "open market operations." And we have recent experience with a larger and broader form of Fed purchases, often called "quantitative easing" (QE): the Fed has exchanged bank money for Treasuries on an unprecedented scale, to encourage low interest rates and increased economic activity. (The Fed has also purchased some other kinds of securities; this analysis focuses on the Fed's activities with Treasury securities.) After the two major rounds of quantitative easing in the past few years, often called QE1 and QE2, interest rates continue to be very low and the actions have clearly not caused excessive lending. Quantitative easing does not purport to create new wealth or new assets for the financial system: it simply provides more of one form of liquid assets held by the private sector - bank deposits - in exchange for another form of highly liquid assets - Treasuries. QE does not provide the overall banking system with more money to lend; as noted in Section 2.1, the banking system does not use deposits to make loans: the system creates new deposits as banks lend. QE does create excess reserves for banks; QE1 increased them on a large scale. This provides additional liquidity for the banking system; some banks may then feel more confident about growing lending. And the increase in excess reserves provides the banking system with greater ability to make loans or buy Treasuries or other assets, since the reserves required on the new deposits created by the banks could easily be drawn from the large pot of excess reserves. By the time of QE2, the banking system already had substantial excess reserves, there was no reserve constraint on the banking system's ability to grow loans, and QE2 did not matter in that regard.

After QE, the amount of Treasuries held by private-sector investors has been reduced by the Fed, which provides bank deposits in exchange, so the overall aggregate portfolio of investors then has slightly more bank credit risk, since the proportion of bank deposits relative to Treasuries has increased. When the Fed buys Treasuries, there is no other direct change in the credit risk or equity risk profile of the aggregate portfolio. The increase in deposits and excess reserves does mean that many investors who previously held more Treasuries now hold bank deposits that could be invested in Treasuries, if there were more Treasuries available. Interest rates on Treasuries are bid down even further due to this larger demand, which is exactly one of the Fed's objectives in QE.

If, as some of the bonds held by the Fed mature, the Fed were simply to allow them to expire, then the deposits and excess reserves created by the Fed's purchase of those bonds would stay in place. But as the Treasury Department redeems bonds and issues new bonds to replace the maturing ones, it essentially delivers deposits from the banking system to the Fed. That process is similar to open market operations for tightening purposes, in which the Fed sells bonds into the market, thus reducing deposits in the banking system and the excess reserves of the banks. If the economy is still slow, the Fed could choose to replace maturing Treasuries by buying more in the market. Or, gradually, as the economy gets stronger, the Fed's holding of Treasury securities can decline, and deposits (the money supply) and excess reserves can decline.

In order to understand the implications of Fed purchase of Treasuries, it is necessary to look at the overall port-folios of financial assets in the system, and especially at the total of highly liquid assets, including deposits and Treasuries. To look at only what is called money would be similar to looking only at savings deposits, or only $20 bills, or any other single component of the total picture. Appendix D illustrates the direct effects of QE on the aggregate financial investment portfolio in USD.[2]

With that full picture, it is difficult to see why Fed purchase of Treasuries would cause inflation. Only what is defined as the money supply has increased, while other "cash equivalent" assets have decreased by the same amount. Suppose an investor owned $10 million in a portfolio including a "cash" component of $2 million: $1 million in the bank and $1 million of Treasuries. After the Fed buys Treasuries, the portfolio contains $1.1 million in the bank and $900,000 of Treasuries. Either way, the

---

2   Since total financial assets are over $150 trillion, even $1.5 trillion of QE would amount to changing the composition of less than 1% of the total, and would not directly affect the total.

highly liquid "cash" component of the portfolio, available for other investment (or spending), is $2mm, 20% of the portfolio. Why would that investor be any more inclined to spend excessively?

risk

There are other, very different circumstances in which rapidly growing money supply could seriously portend inflation: specifically if the money supply were to increase as a result of bank loans growing excessively in a strong economy. The money supply grows automatically as loans are made, but the driving economic force is the use of the proceeds of the loans: as companies and consumers borrow from banks, they typically plan to spend the new money. If overdone, in a hot economy, that could well cause inflation. But that form of increase in the money supply is *very* different from QE. Inflation has remained quite low after QE1 and QE2. In fact, the "national debt" and money supply have grown during the administrations of every president for decades, sometimes rapidly, while inflation in the U.S. has not exceeded 5% for 30 years.

It would actually be possible for the U.S. government, as it makes payments, to just leave the new money in the banking system, rather than issue new Treasuries. That would increase the money supply. Excess reserves of banks would grow beyond the $1.4 trillion that they already hold. Investors would be deprived of the opportunity to invest more of their bank money into safe Treasuries, while banks today would be paid interest on the reserves, by the Fed, at a rate higher than the rate paid on Treasury bills. And it would mean that the Fed, in the future, would likely have to use different tools to control growth of lending. Instead, the U.S. uses Treasuries to finance deficits, rather than creation of new money. The practice of issuing Treasuries, which also provide safe saving opportunities to investors, has worked extremely well for a very long time.

It is important, however, that deficit financing be used to stabilize the economy only during slow economic times. Increased demand by government during strong times could well lead to inflation. That means serious programs to develop reasonably balanced primary budgets for future years when the economy is hoped to be strong. (A "structurally balanced" budget.) Such programs should lead to periods when the economy is growing well, while Treasuries are flat, or increasingly only slightly, and may lead to modest reductions in Treasuries outstanding in especially strong years.

As a practical matter, the backstop of the Fed is extremely unlikely ever to be needed, because investors have deposits they want to invest, and find it more rational to put the extra cash in Treasuries rather than leave it in banks, to the extent that Treasuries are available. The interest rates set by the market reflect current assessments of risk of banks compared to the government guarantee of Treasuries. Over history, whenever times are especially uncertain, the market turns to Treasuries, and Treasury rates are bid further down.

Chapter 3

Why taxes are never needed to "pay off" "national debt"

3.1 Why Treasuries are not like personal debt

People often have misconceptions about Treasury securities ("national debt") because they think of them as similar to personal debt. When people borrow money, they incur real debt, an obligation that must be repaid in full with money earned from another source. Borrowers owe money to their lenders. But "national debt" is not the same as personal debt for countries like America, with their own currencies.

In many ways, applying the term "debt" to Treasuries leads to a number of assumptions that are relevant for individual debt but are simply not applicable to Treasury securities. A number of people seem to be under the impression that, once the government has issued Treasuries to finance a deficit, then taxes in the future would have to be raised enough to "pay off" the money someday. "National debt" is sometimes maligned as inherently "bad" in moral tones, as with a person who incurs debt far beyond his means; issuance of Treasuries is inappro-priately associated with an irresponsible government that cannot earn enough to pay the bills, so has to borrow, and may "go broke." *But none of these concepts are applicable to U.S. Treasuries.*

3.2 Treasuries *are* different

Sometimes people think of Treasuries as a form of "debt" because each bond can be converted to bank dollars at its maturity. But the issuance cycle is really an operational matter. New Treasuries take the place of previous ones, with the same backing of the U.S. government. Only the interest rate changes, and investors continue to hold them as the most reliable USD financial assets. It's very like issuing Treasuries without expiration dates, which simply adjust interest rates to the current market at prede-termined periods: some have their interest rates based on prevailing rates for three months, and the rates reset every three months, by an auction process; others have interest based on market rates for one year or five years, then reset to the then-applicable rates every one year or five years.[1] The concept is essentially that used for long-term (or undated) floating-rate bonds. All these Treasury secu-rities are fully tradable, and the government, which can always create more bank money, can retire any security,

---

1   This concept is similar to that used for certain corporate notes that are rolling, perpetual, tradable instruments.

and change the timing mix of interest-rate resets, through open-market operations. The securities actually issued by the Treasury could be structured technically in such a form, but instead the Treasury uses a system of series of new issues, which does not change the underlying essence.[2] This program has functioned very effectively for hundreds of years, with never any need to "pay off" the aggregate.

We hear some political leaders make statements to the effect that families should not be burdened with more debt, and similarly should not burden our nation with more "national debt." If a family owes a lender $20,000, then the family will need to repay it, essentially giving over $20,000 worth of real goods and services to someone else. It may be very sensible for families to borrow, if they can afford it, to support education, a home, a car, etc., but eventually the debt must be paid back. Treasuries are not like that at all. The people of America will never have to give over $9½ trillion of goods and services to someone else, for what is called "national debt." The ownership of financial assets moves around the U.S. economy, and bank deposits and Treasuries are constantly being exchanged with each other, but the citizens of America do not have to pay the $9½ trillion of Treasuries to "someone else." (We'll address the question of foreign ownership of a portion of U.S. dollar assets in Chapter 6.) Money can

---

2   The Treasury Department has announced that it plans to issue some form of floating-rate notes starting in 2013.

flow out of a family's accounts, but U.S. dollars cannot flow out of the U.S. financial system.

If the government had chosen to fund some of its outlays during slow times with newly created money, we would not hear concerns about how to "pay off" the new money. Instead, the government supports part of its outlays in cold economic times by the issuance of Treasury securities, a different form of new financial assets, which have other advantages, and also do not need to be "paid off."

People generally do not think of banks as "in debt" to depositors, even though the banks are obligated to provide "cash" to them upon demand for checking accounts, and at maturity for term deposits. Of course, banks providing cash, other than paper currency, really means more bank money, still a claim on the banks. Deposits in banks really amount to claims on the banks and their assets such as loans, securities, derivatives, etc., and the production of the companies and people to whom the banks have lent. Treasury bonds represent rights to share in the future production of the United States of America. *What does the US 'produce'?*

3.3 Some Historical Context

The U.S. has a very long experience with Treasuries, which have been outstanding every year since 1791—and that has certainly not prevented America from great progress.

Total Treasuries held by the public have never been fully paid off at any time. During the last 50 years, Treasuries held by the public increased every year except for small reductions in five years. The U.S. has gone through good times and difficult times, and met a great range of challenges, without ever suffering from some form of great "burden" from Treasury securities.

The issue has historically not been simply a partisan matter. The "national debt" has increased during most Democratic and Republican administrations for decades. The last few years of the Clinton administration were exceptional in that the figures were actually reduced in each of those years. During the Reagan administration, "public debt" tripled, and the economy improved substantially. During the recent eight years of the Bush administration, the total Treasuries held by the public roughly doubled.[3] In the Obama administration the figure has grown substantially, as the economy has been gradually recovering from the global financial crisis of 2008.

The amount of Treasuries held by the public increased by a substantial percentage in 1839, but they were not a great burden on the next generation in 1869: the economy was doing fine. Similarly, Treasuries increased in 1933, but were not a great burden to America in 1963: the

---

3   It is often noted that the global financial crisis of 2007, 2008, and 2009 was driven in part by excessive and inappropriate consumer and corporate debt. But that was *private* debt; Treasuries and their counterparts in other nations were used to significantly *mitigate* the severity of the crisis.

economy was in the midst of a strong period of solid growth. Treasuries increased in 1965, but were not a great burden to America in 1995, another time of solid growth. There is no reason to worry that Treasuries issued in 2012 will be a great burden to Americans in 2042. Quite to the contrary, Treasuries have proved extremely useful instruments over the course of American history.

There is no good reason to use the term "debt" at all when referring to total outstanding Treasury securities. The expression "national debt" is really 100 years out of date for America, and does not reflect the modern U.S. financial system. U.S. Treasury securities are unique financial instruments issued by the government, bearing interest at rates reset to market periodically through a very special auction system. That realization leaves us free to explore the real nature of Treasuries, without the preconceptions of "debt" as most people think of it in a personal sense.

3.4 What would it mean to "pay off" all the "national debt"?

All this has to make us wonder why people worry so much about "national debt"? What harm has it caused for America? What burden has it placed on Americans? Despite decades of watching the "national debt clock" with concern, taxes are not higher in order to "pay off the debt" – which we know does not happen. There has been fear of higher interest rates as a result of more Treasuries outstanding, but that is clearly not the case, as interest rates are at exceptionally low levels, despite over a decade of increases in Treasuries outstanding.

The term "pay off" really means to provide bank deposits in exchange for maturing Treasuries. While *individual* Treasury securities are often exchanged for bank deposits at maturity, the *aggregate* total is never "paid off," and there is no need for extra taxes to pay them down.[4]

How could it make sense to try to fully "pay off" Treasuries? Suppose that the government decided to actually embark on a program to "pay off" almost the entirety of Treasuries currently owned by investors – in order to fully eliminate the "great burden for our children." Taxpayers would have to take $9 trillion out of their bank accounts to pay for this; the holders of Treasuries would be paid that amount in exchange for their bonds; the money supply would be unchanged, but there would be a huge movement of money from taxpayers to bondholders. And, the aggregate investors who used to hold $9.5 trillion of Treasuries plus $9 trillion of bank deposits would have their total assets reduced in a very substantial way, leaving only the $9 trillion in the banks and $.5 trillion of Treasuries, compared to

---

4   In very unusual years, the government has run a fiscal surplus, and Treasuries have been reduced, very modestly. In such a year, the government takes somewhat more in taxes than it spends, which is economically helpful only in a year when the economy is overheating, and needs to be cooled down.

the $18.5 trillion of financial assets that they hold now in deposits plus Treasuries. Why ever consider such a program, which is just not necessary? The entire concept of a program to "pay off" of the "national debt" does not make sense. It will never be needed, will never occur, and will never present a great burden to our children.

Many Americans are under the misimpression that they are paying taxes, this year, that are being used to "pay off national debt." In fact, the amount of our tax dollars used to "pay off national debt" this year is zero, last year was zero, and next year will be zero.

And no tax dollars will be required of our children to "pay off national debt."

We have talked ourselves into sustaining an unfounded fear. The real damage to America relating to "national debt" is a result of America's fear of it: we have been too reluctant to take steps that would be good for the nation, as we have been held back by needless fear of increasing the "national debt."

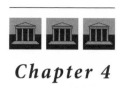

Chapter 4

Why U.S. Treasuries cannot face the same problems as securities issued by eurozone nations

When a specific Treasury security reaches maturity, the U.S. government offers to exchange it at par for USD bank money. Many investors choose to reinvest in new Treasuries immediately, since they are safer financial assets than bank money; investors know that Treasuries do not have bank credit or liquidity risk. Some investors take payment in bank money, for which they have a use at the time.

But a nation in the eurozone issues securities without having its own full central bank, without the ability to create bank money, and in a currency that is not fully its own. In some eurozone countries, such as Greece, a fear of investors is that when a Greek government bond denominated in euros reaches maturity, the Greek government might not be able to provide the investor with bank money in euros in exchange for the bond. That is a genuine concern, because the Greek government has limited availability of euros, and cannot create euros for its banking system. Such a situation cannot occur in the U.S., which has its own currency, Treasury, and central bank, and where the U.S. government can and does create and exchange securities and bank money in U.S. dollars.

The European Central Bank and commercial banks in the eurozone can create bank money in euros, and have done so, but the euros can easily move out of the Greek financial system to other euro nations, and the ECB is not a part of the Greek government.

In the U.S., in contrast, when the government or banks create bank money in USD, that money must stay in the U.S. banking system. The situation of eurozone nations is more like that of states in the USA.

We often see opinions about a theoretical "upper limit" of public "debt to GDP"; sometimes 80 percent is suggested, other times 120 percent, while even others might say 150 percent. The figures are often computed in very different ways. Sometimes the computations use securities held by the public, other times "gross debt," which includes intra-government accounting entries. Usually, indirect debt, such as that of government-owned development banks and "policy" banks, is not included, so it is especially difficult to make good comparisons between countries that use such vehicles heavily or only slightly, if at all. These figures do not have a fundamental compelling logic – except for countries like the eurozone nations. Economists have not discovered a new law of the universe in their laboratories; the figures are just estimates, based on different definitions and opinions. There seems to be little cogent explanation of why a number of countries outside the eurozone are able to operate regularly with relatively higher ratios—sometimes much higher than the limits stated by pundits. Even money is outstanding in vastly different amounts in different countries, and often does not get attention.[1]

In the U.S., the expression "debt held by the public" is used to refer to the totals excluding the "trust funds" that are internal accounting entries relating to programs such as Social Security and Medicare. Figures sometimes used for "gross national debt," computed *including* those accounting entries, are highly misleading. The trust funds do not hold any Treasury bonds that were bought by investors or could be sold in the market. Both the Congressional Budget Office and the Office of Management and Budget have recognized, in various publications, that the trust funds are "accounting mechanisms, not assets of the government, and not relevant for the overall federal budget." The background on trust fund accounting is explained further in Appendix E.

In the U.S., "debt held by the public" is about $11 trillion; dividing that by about $15 trillion in GDP gives a ratio of about 73% for the U.S. The amount of Treasuries

---

1   For example in China the money supply (bank deposits) exceeds 200% of GDP while in the U.S. it's only about 60% of GDP. The total of bank money plus Treasuries in the U.S. amounts to less than 150% of GDP, less than half the comparable figure for China, and there is no concern about the ability of either government to issue bonds in its own currency.

actually held by public investors (non-U.S. government) is about $9.3 trillion: the $11 trillion "public debt" less the roughly $1.7 trillion currently held by the Fed, another part of the U.S. government. Dividing the $9.3 trillion held by investors by about $15 trillion in GDP gives a ratio of about 62% for the U.S.

Japan has a ratio of government bonds to GDP that is reported at over 200%. Despite warnings about the viability of the bond market when the ratio was at 100%, grim warnings when it was 150%, and grimmer warnings when at 200%, Japan has continually been smoothly issuing Japanese Government Bonds ("JGBs"), which are widely traded, and we still read of investors turning to JGBs when there is a "flight to quality." Japan certainly has economic challenges, but during 2010, before the earthquake and tsunami, its GDP grew over 4 percent, it had no inflation, and unemployment was only about 5 percent. Despite all the fears about the 200 percent ratio, the economy of Japan performed in 2010 in a way that would be the envy of most of Europe, as well as America. Japan continually issues new bonds efficiently: all its bonds are in its own currency; it has its own full central bank; and JGBs are always the safest place to invest Japanese Yen.

Overall, the use of such ratios as "debt-to-GDP" provides some general trend data, but very limited insight into the issue, and thus little basis for reaching a meaningful conclusion for a country like the U.S. For the governments of eurozone nations, however, which are more like those of American states than like the USA, the ratios provide part of a set of measures of their ability to service their debt.

The financial systems of eurozone nations have very fundamental differences from the U.S. In Greece or Ireland or Portugal, money (deposits in banks) does not have to stay in the country: it can move, in euros, to any other eurozone country, with differing degrees of government protection. That is a critical difference from the U.S. banking system, in which all USD deposits must remain in the U.S. banking system, with one national deposit insurance program, a national system for problem-bank resolution and one central government there to stabilize the system if needed. In addition to a more unified eurozone banking system, some member nations may need a form of capital controls to keep large amounts of euros from moving to other nations.

The government debt of eurozone nations is a form of debt that is not like U.S. Treasuries. As noted, the situation for debt of eurozone countries is similar to that of states in the USA. But in the U.S., almost all states have some form of balanced-budget requirement, and the states depend primarily on the federal government, financed through federal taxes and issuance of Treasuries, for automatic stabilizers, for added stabilizing steps during weak economic times, and for emergencies. For example, when a hurricane hits some states badly, the

U.S. government provides major aid, financed by U.S. Treasuries. The eurozone faces the challenge of how to properly facilitate such economic stabilization financing, in a system in which national governments do not control their financial systems.

The eurozone does not have a zone-wide risk-free financial asset, similar to Treasuries in the U.S. Perhaps bonds issued by the ECB, which is the backer of euro currency and has the ability to create euros, might fill that role.

These are critical differences that affect the government debt of eurozone nations in ways that just do not apply to U.S. Treasuries.

Chapter 5

Why we do not need to worry about interest rates on Treasuries (The myth of the "bond vigilantes")

Treasury auctions always sell all the securities offered; as explained in earlier chapters, investors always have sufficient funds at the time of each Treasury offering, and Treasuries are always the safest investment for U.S. dollars. The interest rates on new bills and bonds are set by the market, through an auction process. For years, questions have been raised about whether some investors (often called "bond vigilantes") could conclude that there is too much government "debt," and demand much higher interest rates specifically for Treasuries. But despite the catchy expression "bond vigilantes," there are always enough bank deposits (and excess reserves that banks can use to create more deposits) to exchange for the new Treasuries. Some investors will have to decide whether to hold bank money or Treasuries; the Treasuries are always lower risk than bank deposits, and thus will always warrant interest rates below the bank rates for each maturity.[1] Treasury auctions allocate a limited supply of new Treasury securities to bidders who want to invest in the safety and liquidity of Treasuries.

The myth of the bond vigilantes forcing Treasury rates up has been around for years. Every year for the past decade at least, experts have predicted "this is the year the bond vigilantes will catch up with our rising 'national debt' and force up rates on Treasuries," but every year the interest rates have remained low. Currently, after years of increasing Treasuries outstanding, Treasury rates are at extraordinarily low levels. The myth about bond vigilantes forcing up Treasury rates has been seen, year after year, to be just a myth.

There may be bond vigilantes actively riding in the eurozone, for reasons that apply to those nations but not to the U.S., as explained in Chapter 4. Underlying demand for U.S. Treasuries is extremely large; even a small increase in yields can generate very substantial amounts of bidding for new issues. Also, as noted in Chapter 2, banks can buy very large amounts of Treasuries. If, in some very unusual time, Treasury rates moved up just slightly above corresponding bank interest rates, banks would have clear incentives to buy Treasuries, which are considered risk-free investments, and banks could invest without impairing their regulatory capital ratios.

---

1   It is always possible to have temporary fluctuations, as a result of traders' views that are not based on fundamentals, but the fundamental role of U.S. Treasuries in the financial system must prevail.

Interest rates can change for reasons that affect a whole range of financial assets: because the economy seems to be doing better or worse; because people perceive more or less credit risk for banks or companies, or inflation risk; as a result of weather and international commodity fluctuations; because corporate notes and bonds reflect changing risk/return preferences of different investors; because the Fed takes some action; or because there is more or less competition for real goods and services.[2] If the expression "bond vigilante" is used more broadly, it might refer to the market tightening overall, for such reasons. Interest rates could rise (or fall) generally, for banks, Treasuries, corporate bonds, and other instruments, as a result of such factors, but *not* specifically for Treasuries, and *not* because of the total amount of "national debt."

Inflation expectations could be related to anticipated government *expenditures*. For example, if investors see no progress on fixing the budget challenges for 2022, and see government sponsored health care costs rising to a very high percentage of GDP, then they will see more risk of inflation in ten years, and rates on all sorts of bonds of maturities of about ten years or more will go up. Such a rate increase, however, would *not* be caused by the total

---

2   Actions by the Fed might lead to some change in the interest rate profile of the public, depending on the mix of Treasuries issued or retired or purchased or sold by the Fed, so for example, 10-year rates and short-term rates might shift differently. The Fed has its own intentional version of this in what has been called "Operation Twist."

amount of Treasuries outstanding now or next year or ten years from now.

Actually, the real risk is the other way around from the bond vigilante myth: there is no risk to the process of rational investors exchanging bank money for safer Treasuries at competitive rates. But from time to time, depositors become concerned about the safety of their banks and their deposits. Sometimes there are runs on banks, and people withdraw large amounts of paper currency. The "bond vigilantes" don't show up in the U.S., but the "bank vigilantes" do. Depositors try to buy more Treasuries than are available, and rates on Treasuries are bid way down.

Any time investors change their views about degrees of risks, there will be some readjustments in relative rates that affect the rates on various instruments. But Treasuries always reflect the lowest possible risk for USD assets, regardless of the amount of Treasuries outstanding.

Chapter 6

Why interest on Treasuries is not a problem for the U.S.

Interest paid on Treasury securities is fundamentally different than the vast majority of government expenditures: interest does not consume economic resources. For many years, economists have distinguished between the total deficit of a government and its "primary deficit," which refers to the budget deficit excluding payment of interest on Treasuries; the primary deficit is a more meaningful measure of government use of the nation's economic resources.

If the economy is running with substantial unemployment, then it is better for the government to issue more Treasuries to pay for its needs rather than raise taxes. That includes paying interest on existing Treasuries by issuing new Treasuries. There is no more or less money in the system, on a net basis, and no need for additional taxes.

In the rare cases when the economy is hot, at full employment, then the strong economy might produce enough government revenue to pay interest in cash. Would it make much difference in the overall economy? Not likely. Interest paid by the Treasury is income to the public holders of Treasuries, who have financial assets and are often trying to build wealth, rather than spending most of it in the year it was earned.[1] And, in a very strong economy, the government could well run an overall budgetary surplus, as it did in 1999. So, in a weak economy, the payment of interest by issuance of Treasuries could be somewhat helpful, while in a very strong economy, the interest would not be a significant factor overall, and total Treasuries outstanding might actually be reduced.

The payment of interest does not consume any resources, or directly change GDP. These are key reasons why economists have often focused on the primary deficit.[2] Interest on Treasuries is different by nature from real government spending on goods and services, and should not be included in the economic computation of government expenditures; interest does not pay for production, or pay doctors or hospitals for medical services, or provide cash for people who are likely to spend most of it, such as those living on Social Security or on unemployment benefits. The primary deficit, which excludes

---

1   The Federal Reserve has estimated the "wealth effect"—the likely increase in spending resulting from an increase in wealth—at about 3 to 10 percent of the increase in wealth.

2   There is a private-sector analog in the use of "EBITDA" by professional investors looking at company financials. The first initials stand for "Earnings Before Interest."

interest paid, is a more meaningful economic measure of deficits in the US.[3]

Interest payments also do not affect the money supply. Suppose that the Treasury pays $100 of interest from its Fed account. That $100 becomes cash inflow to the holders of Treasury securities. If $20 is paid back to the government as income taxes, investors will be left with a $80 increase in their deposit accounts. The Treasury then issues $80 of new securities, with investors placing the $80 from their bank accounts into Treasuries, and the Treasury fully replenishes its account at the Fed with that $80 plus the $20 of tax revenue. The system is in full balance. The money supply has not changed.

In 2011, the net interest expense for U.S. Treasuries was about $200 billion. What difference would it have made if that cost had been $100 billion less? The gross deficit, including interest, would have fallen from $1.3 trillion to $1.2 trillion, but there would have been no change in the real expenditures of $3.6 trillion. $100 billion less would have been distributed to investors holding Treasury securities, and investors would have bought $100 billion less in new Treasuries. The primary deficit, the difference between revenue and the purchase of actual goods and services would have been unaffected, at about $1.1 trillion. There would have been no reduction in real

---

3   This has been noted by a number of commentators, including Francis X. Cavanaugh, a former Treasury official, in his 1996 book *The Truth about the National Debt*.

purchases by the government, no change in government consumption of economic resources, and no effect on the money supply.

A number of commentators have raised questions about the ability of some eurozone countries to handle interest payments over time. The concern is that, even if the structural primary deficit could be eliminated during a good economy, high real interest payments might continually lead to higher interest costs relative to real GDP, and some eurozone nations might not be able to cope. Mathematically, such a problem could arise if real GDP growth were especially small relative to the real cost of interest on government securities —but it is specific to eurozone countries, or other countries that raise bank money in currencies that are not fully their own. It is not a concern for the U.S., for the fundamental reasons explained in Chapter 2, and because of the U.S. financial system differences from the eurozone, discussed in Chapter 4. The U.S. does not have the risk of escalation that is an issue for some eurozone nations.

In the U.S., interest paid on Treasuries is a small percentage of GDP, and real GDP growth over long periods of time has averaged about the same as the real interest rates for Treasuries. At the time of this writing, the U.S. economy was growing at a real annual rate estimated to be about 2 percent, while three-month Treasuries have a nominal interest rate of less than 10 basis points (one tenth of one percent!). Five-year Treasuries yield less than 1 percent nominally, and much less in terms of real (inflation-adjusted) rates, since inflation has been running about 2 to 3 percent. Even though GDP growth in America is currently quite slow, Treasury rates are even lower – *very* different from conditions in several of the eurozone countries. Current real costs of interest to the Treasury are actually *negative*: the real interest cost to the Treasury is less than zero.

So, there is no need to be concerned about interest on Treasuries, which can always be supported by issuance of relatively small amounts of new securities, and cannot present the problems facing eurozone countries. Since the interest payments do not consume economic resources, the primary deficit, which excludes interest, is a more meaningful measure of government use of economic resources.

Chapter 7

Why foreign ownership
of Treasuries is not a problem

Countries that sell more goods and services to the U.S. than they buy from the U.S. end up with trade surpluses in U.S. dollars, which *must* be held in USD assets. There are only three things they can do with the dollars: buy American goods and services; invest in USD assets; or exchange dollars for another currency—in which case the new owner of the dollars will have choices one or two.

People sometimes speak of China and Japan "sitting on a pile of dollars" and "lending" money to America, but in truth, nations with dollar trade surpluses *must* keep those dollars in the U.S., either by buying American goods and services or by holding dollar assets like U.S. Treasuries. When oil is sold in dollars, the oil-producing nations either spend the dollars or invest them in USD assets, and the dollars ultimately go to either buying American goods and services or investment in the U.S. – often in Treasuries. Some nations hold dollars as a reserve currency with the expectation that others will always want dollars, but when they do, the dollars remain in America. When a foreign bank receives dollars, it really means that bank has dollars on deposit with an American bank. All the dollars paid by Americans to companies, people, governments, or investors in other countries stay in the U.S. financial system. It is not possible for foreign nations to take dollars out of the U.S. financial system.[1]

Sometimes, we hear concerns that having a portion of U.S. Treasuries owned by foreigners might put the U.S. at risk if the foreign investors should decide to sell some of their Treasuries or to buy other assets instead of new Treasury securities. But there is no need for Americans to worry about the proportion of Treasuries owned by foreigners. Foreign entities with trade surpluses in dollars often choose to invest them in assets with minimal risk: U.S. Treasury securities. Investment in U.S. Treasuries is extremely broad around the world and is the primary choice for investors who want the safest places for their dollars. If some foreign owners of dollar bank accounts opt this month to buy some more corporate bonds or UK bonds, for example, instead of Treasuries, then their dollars will be transferred to the current owners of the corporate or UK bonds, who will then have the dollars in their bank accounts, and will then be faced with the decision of what to do with the dollars; along the market

---

1   For a more extensive explanation, see Chapter 1 of *Six Myths.*

chain someone who wants low-risk USD assets will decide to invest it in Treasury securities.

The Treasury market is very, very big and deep. The largest foreign owners of Treasuries might, in a month, increase their holdings by a total of about $25 billion. During that month, typically $10 *trillion* of Treasuries will be traded.

There are large amounts of international assets owned by Americans as well as U.S. assets owned by foreigners: while foreigners own nearly $23 trillion of American assets, including the international reserves that many countries hold in U.S. dollars, Americans own more than $20 trillion of foreign assets. So, foreigners own about a net $3 trillion of USD assets (out of a total of about $200 trillion); that amount can be in many forms: deposits in U.S. banks, Treasuries, corporate bonds, stocks, real estate, etc. If some foreign investors decide to shift their mix of U.S. dollar assets, it just means that U.S. domestic investors exchange some other USD assets for some USD assets owned by foreigners. The proportion held at any time in Treasuries or any other class of assets by any particular set of investors does not really matter.

There are some related issues that *do* warrant attention. With a trade deficit, the U.S. gets the benefits of low-cost imported goods, but other nations accumulate dollars that they can use to purchase American goods and services in the future. This cumulative trade deficit is not a function of Treasury securities; it is a result of trade imbalances that may build up foreign holdings of many types of USD assets, regardless of the proportion that is held at any time by foreigners in Treasuries or other particular forms of USD assets. Restrictive trade practices, such as non-tariff import barriers in some nations, and oil cartels, may contribute to inappropriately high trade deficits for the U.S. The complex issue of the U.S. trade deficit, including imported oil, is an important public policy matter, but does not drive the analysis of the roles of money and Treasuries in the U.S. financial system.

There is also a practical issue as we think about holders of large amounts of U.S. Treasuries: how else might they keep their dollars safe and liquid? China and Japan have each accumulated large amounts of USD reserves from trade surpluses over the years; some they have invested in long-term risk assets around the world; they have also decided to keep a substantial block in safe, highly liquid form: each holds over $1 trillion of U.S. Treasuries. If, hypothetically, one of those nations decided they did not want to hold Treasury securities, it would be extraordinarily difficult for them to find a good place to park so much money in safe and liquid form. They could deposit it in U.S. banks, but that would mean taking bank risk on a very large scale; it's one thing for a big depositor to leave $10 million or even $100 million in a major bank, but quite a different thing to deposit $100 *billion*. As noted above, if the Treasuries were sold to investors in other countries then someone else would end up with the same dollars and the same questions. And a large investor who traded dollars for other currencies would face more serious issues: there are certainly lots of questions about large holdings of euros; and the bonds of other nations do not have nearly the breadth and depth of the U.S. Treasury market. Where could an investor holding over $1 trillion turn, other than to Treasuries, for safety and liquidity? Major foreign holders of dollars really need U.S. Treasuries.

Whenever holders of Treasuries sell some of those securities, they receive bank-account dollars that have to be invested somewhere in the USD financial system. Every day, some investors are selling some of the lowest-risk USD assets (Treasuries) and buying higher-risk dollar assets, while other investors are selling higher-risk assets and buying low-risk assets, notably Treasuries. In the open financial system of the U.S., different investors continually vary allocations to various dollar assets, in light of changing risk/reward views of large numbers of market participants. Treasuries are always key parts of overall USD investment portfolios, and provide benchmarks for the pricing and trading of many financial instruments. There is no need for America to be concerned about the proportion of foreign-owned USD assets that are held in the safest form - U.S. Treasuries.

Chapter 8

The "debt limit" debate in Congress

We often hear public statements about how "irresponsible" it is for us to incur deficits in the present, issuing Treasuries that will become "great burdens to future generations of Americans." This concern has been voiced repeatedly in the great debates regarding the "debt limit" or "debt ceiling" – the process by which a new law is passed from time to time, raising the total allowed amount of "national debt." This limit, oddly, is not about the setting of new budgets; it applies to Treasuries to be issued to fulfill contracts and other obligations already incurred by the government. This chapter looks inside the debate statements, and explains why withholding or even delaying increase in this limit would present great risk of financial system crisis.

8.1 The Myth About Increased Taxes to "Pay off Debt"

One key assertion often made in these debates, by those who argue against increasing the limit, is that an increase will force Americans to pay more taxes to "pay off the debt." Chapter 3 explains why that assertion is unfounded. The U.S. has had Treasury securities outstanding every year since 1791, has *never* "paid off" the total outstanding, and will never have to. The U.S. financial system, including Treasuries, is always in balance, regardless of the amount of Treasuries held by the public; investors receiving U.S. dollars for maturing Treasuries must put the dollars in the U.S. financial system. As explained in Chapter 4, this is very different from securities issued by eurozone countries, where euros redeemed in one country can be reinvested in another country.

8.2 There is No Budgeting to Pay Off the "National Debt"

Although there are often comments about "the great burden" of past and current deficits, the people responsible for budget preparation do not actually plan for a process to "pay off" of all outstanding Treasuries. In all the debates about the federal budget plans over the coming years, there has been, appropriately, a great deal of focus on how to reduce the annual deficit and someday be able to balance the primary structural budget in hoped-for years of full employment ten years in the future; and there is focus, *in*appropriately, on the cumulative budget over 10 years. Even in a slow economy, Washington habitually focuses on measures this year or next to "pay down" the cumulative deficit of the next ten years. But that approach takes future projections of good times - with a "hot" economy, when deficit spending would be counterproductive - and drags it to today, when the economy is quite a bit cooler and very much in need of spending. This ten- year cumulative concept is akin to planning for a hot summer next August by turning on the air conditioning now, in January.

The terms "hot" and "cool" economies have real-world implications, just as increases or cuts to government spending have real effects. It makes as little sense to cut a deficit in a weak economy as it does to don down jackets in a heat wave, whatever future weather you expect.

In any case, the attention to the ten-year cumulative total does not include any "pay off" of the current amount of Treasuries outstanding. There is never any serious attention given to a proposal for raising taxes/reducing expenditures enough to create a surplus sufficient to "pay off" the Treasuries currently in public hands.[1] Official budget planners (independent budgeters and those of

---

1   The debate is further confused by the fact that legislative limit is computed using not only the amount of Treasuries "held by the public" (about $11 trillion), but also about $4.5 trillion from what are really just accounting entries for Social Security and other government "trust funds" - as explained in Chapter 4.

both major political parties) simply do not plan for "paying off" the outstanding Treasuries from deficits and Treasury issuance of the past; they know that it is not necessary and will never happen.

8.3 Toying with Financial System Crisis

Failure to raise the "ceiling" when the U.S. is near the limit specified in prior legislation would mean that the government could not issue more Treasuries, and would not have enough cash to pay all its obligations. The government would then have to decide which existing promises to meet in full, which to pay partially, and which to defer for the future. As often interpreted, that cash shortfall would mean that the Treasury might not be able to pay interest legally due on maturing Treasuries, and would not be able to issue new Treasuries to cover the interest.

Thinking of using a "debt ceiling" to prevent the Treasury from paying interest as it becomes due on Treasury securities reflects an extremely unrealistic, even dangerous, view of the financial system. Keep in mind that the total amount of Treasuries held by investors is more than the entirety of bank deposits in America. Treasuries represent trillions of dollars of savings by Americans. No responsible legislature can seriously threaten those savings and the whole financial system. Suppose that a law were passed preventing every bank in America from paying interest on deposits, including the interest already promised to depositors. Each bank would in effect be in default of its obligations to depositors. Imagine the uproar from millions of consumers and businesses! If Treasuries actually were prevented, by law, from fully paying interest due for maturing securities, it would throw the entire financial system into turmoil in a very short time. If Treasuries were considered technically in default, banks in every part of the nation (actually the world) would be affected: banks hold large amounts of Treasuries (and related securities), which, if in technical default, could seriously impair capital and credit standing of many banks, could impair their ability to use collateral to borrow from the Fed, could interrupt their ability to complete many thousands of transactions in which Treasuries are used, and could lead to bank runs, potentially even panic. Securities firms, money-market funds and thousands of companies with holdings of Treasuries directly or in pension funds, and with deposits at banks that would then be in crisis, would be in financial turmoil. Millions of consumer and business transactions would be frozen, there would likely be liquidity panics for money-market funds in addition to runs on banks and securities firms. Possibly, maybe, the Fed could provide enough liquidity to hold off the panic temporarily. But it would not take long before the virtual freezing of the financial system, the disruption and threat to the savings of millions of people, the stoppages of daily commerce, and the fears of ordinary citizens and businesses, would create such huge pressure on legislators that they would need to go into emergency session, with much egg on their faces, to raise the limit. The limit would surely be lifted, and the question would then be how long and hard it would be to repair the extensive damage that had been foolishly and needlessly inflicted on the nation's financial system by our own legislators.

The Treasury *may* have a route that might be used in such an emergency, although many other obligations would still have to go unpaid or partially paid until the ceiling was lifted. The government could decide, in light of the tremendous harm threatened to the financial system and economy if Treasury securities were not serviced, to give interest payments high priority in the use of available cash flow. Such a program could keep Treasuries fully current, and that policy could, possibly, avoid the financial crisis.[2]

Of course, as we've seen in earlier chapters of this book, there really is no "national debt" in a traditional sense; there is exchange of one form of government-backed financial instrument (Treasuries) with another form of financial instrument (bank deposits). There is no sense in disrupting this exchange process which is such an integral part of the financial system.

What *is* appropriate for government focus is *spending*

---

2   The 14th amendment to the constitution has been cited by some experts as supporting such a policy by the Treasury.

and taxation, rather than "national debt." There are important but very different questions about how to manage primary deficits, and thus minimize excess demand on resources *during very strong economic times in the future.* But the spending and taxation questions should be debated as part of the budget approval process, not in a "debt limit" battle that could curtail the government's ability to fully pay obligations already approved and made, one which threatens major disruption to the entire financial system. And, as earlier chapters have explained, issuance of Treasuries to support a larger deficit this year, in an economy of high unemployment, will *not* cause great burdens for the future.

8.4 Rating Agency Views

Views of the major rating agencies often have attention in the press. Some of them have expressed concerns about U.S. Treasury securities, particularly regarding the political uncertainties. It is important to put these views in perspective. If a rating agency is giving advice to a global investor who could be in any currency, then, for example, an agency might believe that Swiss government bonds, denominated in Swiss Francs, are safer than U.S. Treasuries in dollars, largely because of the political uncertainties in the U.S. But it is a different question when viewing the position of Treasuries from the perspective of someone who is an investor in U.S. dollars. The rating agencies are evaluating probability of default. But, as explained in the previous section, if Treasuries were to default, no financial asset in the U.S., including money in banks, could escape very substantial problems, because defaulted Treasuries would be so disruptive for the entire U.S. financial system. Treasuries define the base for USD financial assets. The U.S. government, which can and does create U.S. dollars, can and must maintain the integrity of Treasuries in order to maintain the viability of the entire financial system.

Chapter 9

Economic Saving and Treasuries

Okay, most of the things we hear about "national debt" (U.S. Treasuries) are not true. Then what *are* the implications of Treasury issuance for the economy?

Economic Saving and productive Investment

Running a budget deficit in a weak economy is generally helpful, because reduced taxes should induce increased consumption and production, or because the government will directly purchase production (such as road improvements) or distribute more cash to people who are likely to purchase new production and services. But as we have seen in earlier chapters, the deficit will not reduce the amount of cash in the system; issuance of Treasuries does not consume money from the financial system. Deficits have no direct effect on real economic Saving or Investment; government deficits always mean equal increases in private-sector Saving.

Analysis in Chapter 3 of *Six Myths* explains that attempts to increase economic Saving cannot result in increased economic Investment, and that it is really business actions to increase Investment that lead to a rise in national Saving. But, before making substantial Investments in new factories and equipment, businesses generally need to see increases in demand coming for their products and services.

Government can influence the overall market environment, but in a free-market economy, the level of economic Saving or Investment is determined largely by private-sector Investment in productive assets such as factories, equipment, software, and buildings. (Government can and does build infrastructure. In the U.S., that is counted as Government *spending*, not Investment. In some countries, including China, the government directly initiates some infrastructure projects that are classified as Investment, which also results in economic Saving.)

9.2 Heat and Air Conditioning

There is nothing "wrong" with deficits in a slow economy. Quite to the contrary, it would be irresponsible to try to balance the budget during slow economic times with high unemployment, just as it would be irresponsible not to plan for how to keep the primary budget reasonably balanced during strong times of low unemployment and high capacity utilization in the future. Heat is useful in the winter, air conditioning useful in the summer. Insisting on a single deficit-reduction policy applicable at all times would be like insisting that air-conditioning is always right and proper, even when the temperature falls to 20°F and heat is clearly needed.

In the unfortunately rare times of low unemployment and high capacity utilization, collecting taxes roughly equal to government expenditures is part of the system of resource allocation in the economy, and helps avoid excessive inflation. But in slow, cool times, with the economy running well below capacity, the key issue is not one of economic demand potentially exceeding production; the challenge is how to get demand and production higher. At such times it is neither necessary nor appropriate for government expenditures and revenue to be equal. The next question is how to finance government expenditure above its revenue. The government could just create the money to spend; that would be simple but would have some disadvantages, as noted in Chapter 2. It has worked well over many years for the government to use financial instruments with their own built-in investment characteristics, which do not increase the "money supply": U.S. Treasuries. New financial assets are created, and that leads to the next topic.

9.3 Value-Added

The overall value of assets in a nation is related to future production and utility. If new claims were introduced without sufficiently offsetting future increases in production or other value, then the real value of pre-existing assets might decline, perhaps through inflation over time.[1] But as long as the level of production is increased sufficiently, or asset values are otherwise increased, then the real value of existing claims should remain stable, or increase; and the new total of value of assets should reflect increased total wealth for the nation.

Funds from issuance of Treasuries can produce a wide scope of added value as a result of government support for the economy in slow times. Increased GDP (production and sales) and increased employment should help the overall value of many assets; improved profits from increased sales, for example, should raise the value of stocks in the market; and deficit spending used for development of infrastructure and education should improve the future productivity of the nation, which should increase overall asset values over time.

There is also the benefit from the multiplier effect. Transactions in modern economies result in *sequences* of effects. Those who are paid for work on infrastructure

---

1   An extreme example, for illustration: Suppose that taxes were reduced for a segment of the population who spent very little of the tax reductions, and saved almost all, resulting in very little productive gains at the time. That would not cause inflation at the time, since there would be no increased demand. If those savers decided to spend some of that savings in a future year of a slow economy, that should not cause inflation. But if the savers decided to spend during a strong year of low unemployment and high capacity utilization, there would be inflationary pressure at that point.

projects then buy a range of goods and services; those who are paid for those transactions then buy more, etc. The chain of transactions generates added GDP above the original amount, perhaps resulting in a total 1.5 to 2 times the original amount spent. The size of the multiplier factor for various situations is debated by economists, but it will add in some degree to the real economic benefit of such programs, and will very likely add to business sales volumes, profits, stock valuations, and even to government tax revenues.

In all cases, there is no burden of increased taxes on future generations in America to "pay off" Treasuries.

9.4 Spending Wisely

The government does have an important responsibility to spend wisely. We clearly should strive not to issue Treasuries to finance activities with no productive or other value. Neither government nor the private sector can be expected to be perfectly efficient, but the more productive programs clearly provide more economic and societal value. Slow economic periods are times for attention to programs to build for the future, such as infrastructure – without fear of "the national debt." In such times, like 2012 and 2013, many of the best minds of our nation should be focused on the careful selection, management, and completion of government projects that will support the economy in the short run and will add long-run value for the nation.

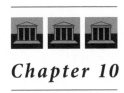

Chapter 10

Conclusions

We have now seen:

- That "national debt" is an expression for the total of U.S. Treasury securities held by investors.
- That "money" is really "bank money," created largely by banks, subject to bank risk, and thus not as safe as Treasuries, which are fully backed by the U.S. government;
- How Treasuries serve as safe repositories of large amounts of savings for millions of investors;
- How Treasuries are unique financial instruments, not like personal debt;
- How Treasuries in aggregate are never "paid off," and will not require taxes to "pay off" in the future;
- Why U.S. Treasuries cannot face the same problems as securities issued by eurozone nations;
- Why the ratios of government securities to GDP might be useful in looking at eurozone countries, but not the U.S.;

- Why interest rates on Treasuries do not rise just because there are more Treasuries outstanding;

- Why foreign ownership of Treasuries does not create indebtedness to other nations, and does not present a big risk to America;

- How interest paid on Treasuries does not consume economic resources, and why the "primary deficit," excluding interest, is especially meaningful;

- Why the "debt ceiling" debates cannot sustainably negate the value of Treasuries, but risk major disruptions to the entire financial system;

- Why there is no need to "pay for" near-term deficits over future years – a process that could well be counterproductive as the economy recovers;

- Why Washington's focus on reducing the cumulative deficit over ten years is misplaced, not helpful, and likely damaging to the economy;

- Why deficit policy should vary under different conditions: Heat is useful in the winter, air conditioning useful in the summer; why programs to control deficits ten years from now, when we hope the economy will be hot, are important. And why none of these issues need be influenced by concern over the myth of "national debt."

In light of all this understanding – driven by analysis, not ideology - it becomes clear that referring to Treasuries as "national debt" is really neither meaningful nor useful. Treasuries are unique government financing instruments that provide safe financial assets for savings for millions of investors.

So, with these realizations, *we become free of fear of "national debt."* Treasury securities are real, of course, but we do not need to fear them and should not let concern about them dominate our considerations of economic policies.

The main point of this book is to free people's thinking from the constraints of the old views of Treasuries, money, and especially "national debt." Then, reasonable discussion can lead to practical alternatives in the best interests of our nation, which currently suffers with a persistently very slow economy and high unemployment. This author believes that the major, primary driver for the U.S. economy should continue to be and will be the vibrant private sector of America. A key responsibility of government is to foster an economic environment that is conducive to private-sector success. But when the private sector does not produce enough jobs or growth, then government needs to step in, providing stabilization and assistance: heat in the cold months. There have been far too many times when slow economies were too meekly addressed, were far too slow to get better by themselves, and did not produce jobs when spending was cut. And there have been a number of times when various governments – including those of Franklin Roosevelt and Ronald Reagan – took active fiscal steps to help the economy, including increased spending and reduced taxes, which did reduce unemployment and increase GDP - financed, appropriately, by issuance of Treasury securities.

Government has the obligation to pursue efficiency of its activities; to avoid needless intrusion into private lives and private sector business; to develop and implement balanced systems of taxation and regulation that do not needlessly impede American initiative and progress; and to make sound and wise choices about government-sponsored projects that can provide modern infrastructure for the American private sector to be successful in an internationally competitive world. Policymakers may have differing views on the extent and nature of heat that government should provide when the economy is very cold. That debate and compromise process can be healthy; but I hope that those involved read this book and do not base their views on misunderstanding of how money and Treasuries work and on false fears about "national debt" in United States of America.

There are important issues of this nature coming up for America. Some policymakers oppose another year extension of the reduced rate on payroll taxes due to unfounded concern that it would contribute to the "national debt problem." Unwarranted fear of "national debt" is a factor in the debate about how to address the high risk to the economy from the tax increases and spending reductions preprogrammed to start in 2013 (the "fiscal cliff"). And much attention is focused, *inappropriately,* on "paying for" near-term deficits, and reducing the growth of "national debt" cumulatively over ten years. Programs to reduce the *future annual* deficits expected ten years from now, in the robust economy hoped for in 2022, *do* need to be implemented. But, as explained in this book, "national debt" is not what it is typically painted to be; and concern over the amount of Treasuries outstanding should *not* stand in the way of helping the economy and employment in 2013.

America does not need to fear "national debt," and has great opportunities at this time. We can create millions of new jobs, substantially reducing America's persistent high unemployment. We can repair and modernize the roads, bridges, dams, electrical grids, airports, schools, and military equipment of America. And taxes can be reduced at the same time.

It is time to turn off the "national debt clocks." Better still, the clocks can be changed to measure something more meaningful, such as the number of productive work hours lost this year by Americans who are looking for jobs that the economy is not creating.

There is no need to live with the sadness of high unemployment and burden of low growth just because of worry over "national debt." We have the opportunity to grow much more strongly, and to build a far better future. America has faced challenges many times before and tackled them with ingenuity and spirit, accomplishing great things. America has the means to deal with great challenges, when it sees them clearly, unclouded by needless fear.

Appendix

A. Illustration of Banking System Loan & Deposit Growth (referred from Chapter 2)

As noted in Section 2.1 - How Deposits Grow, there are often misunderstandings about how the total amounts of deposits grow in an economy and a banking system. The main source of growth of deposits in a nation comes from the banks, which *create* money as they make loans.

Let's look at an overall rough picture of the aggregate balance sheet for all banks in the U.S. Then, we'll add $500 billion of new loans.

Assets	$trillion	Liabilities & Equity	
Loans	7.1	Deposits	8.9
Required reserves at Fed	0.1	Other	2.5
Excess reserves	1.4		
Other	4.2	Equity	1.4
Total	12.8	**Total**	12.8

After making another $500bn of new loans:

Loans	7.6	Deposits	9.4
Required reserves at Fed	0.11	Other	2.5
Excess reserves	1.39		
Other	4.2	Equity	1.4
Total	13.3	**Total**	13.3

So, loans and deposits both grow by $500 billion. There is no way that existing deposits can be used to "fund" new loans. The deposit accounts of the new borrowers are increased by the amounts of their loans, and the banks' obligations to the existing depositors cannot be erased. A small portion of excess reserves now are reclassified at the Fed as required reserves, related to the new deposits.

For an individual bank:

Assets	$billion	Liabilities & Equity	
Loans	100	Deposits	120
Required reserves at Fed	1	Other	46
Excess reserves	20		
Other	59	Equity	14
Total	180	**Total**	180

After making another $10bn of new loans:

Loans	110	Deposits	130
Required reserves at Fed	1.1	Other	46
Excess reserves	19.9		
other	59	Equity	1.4
Total	190	**Total**	190

If the market shares of this bank are stable, then some of its deposits will flow out over time to other banks, while some deposits will flow in from other banks, and its balance sheet should be reasonably stable. If this bank loses net deposits to other banks, then it could use some of its excess reserves to fund the required transfer to the other banks. If the bank is concerned that it might lose a meaningful amount of net deposits, and thus need more cash, it could sell some of its bond portfolio to generate more excess reserves. And, it might undertake a special effort to try to gain deposit market share, taking deposits from other banks, and receiving excess deposits in its Fed account; but the total deposits of the banking system would be unaffected.

Similarly, depositors cannot move money out of the banking system as a whole. If some investors use some of their deposits to buy other assets, such as stocks, then the money in the buyers' deposit accounts moves to the bank accounts of the sellers, and the total money supply is unaffected.

There is a common misconception that the banking system can "fund" new loans with the use of new deposits. That is not possible. If the Fed adds to total deposits through open market operations or "QE," then deposits of the bond sellers increase, and the Fed adds to the excess reserve accounts of the sellers' banks. But those funds in aggregate can be used only in the banks' reserve accounts at the Fed. If a bank makes a new loan, it can use those new funds only to support the required reserves on the new deposits created when the loan is made. If a bank buys a bond from the market, it creates a new deposit in the deposit account of the seller of the bond. Again, the funds provided from QE can be used only to support the required reserves for the new deposits. If the reserve requirements average about 2%, then $1 trillion of new loans and bond purchases by banks would use only $20 billion of the total deposits created by QE.

B. Illustration of Treasury payment/issuance cycle on aggregate portfolio of investment (Referred from Chapter 2)

Consider a case in which the Treasury makes payments for Social Security, federal payroll, contractors, etc. from its Fed account in a total amount of $3. The recipients then deposit those funds in their banks; the money supply is temporarily increased. The money then changes hands, moving through the financial system into various accounts and funds. Then the Treasury issues new bills or notes to investors totaling $3, consisting of $2 of short-term securities and $1 of a longer-term security. This issue is net of any redemption of maturing bills. The Treasury then uses the funds to replenish its account at the Fed. The Treasury has distributed and raised the same amount of money, so there is no change in the money supply.

So, (aside from other market changes, such as stock volatility):

Aggregate balances for USD portfolio managers, investors, savers:

	Before Treasury actions $	After payments, but before new issue $	After payments & new issue $
U.S. Stocks	250	250	250
U.S. Corporate and other bonds	150	150	150
Real Estate	100	100	100
Alternative Investments	100	100	100
International investments	100	100	100

"Cash and equivalents":	300	303	303
Bank checking and savings deposits	100	103	100
Bank time deposits	50	50	50
Treasuries – short-term	100	100	102
Treasury bonds	50	50	51

The adjustment process may take some time, as transactions work their way through the system.

Total financial assets have increased, and there are some small changes in composition and maturity mix, but there is no change in the money supply or in equity risk or credit risk.

C. Illustration of Bank Investment in Treasuries (referred from Chapter 2)

There is no change in the money supply when general investors buy new Treasury securities. But the process is somewhat different if banks are the buyers, and banks can purchase very large amounts.

Suppose the Treasury disburses $10 billion from its Fed account. Deposits in banks, thus the money supply, increase by $10 billion temporarily, as do the reserves of the banking system. If reserve requirements are about 2%[1], banks transfer $200 million of excess reserves at the Fed to their required reserve accounts, so net excess reserves are up by $9.8 billion at that point.

Then the Treasury issues $10 billion of new securities.

---

1   Reserve requirements in the U.S. vary by type of deposit, from zero to 10%, and currently average less than 2%.

If general investors buy the Treasuries (exchange bank money for new Treasuries), then deposits in banks are reduced by $10 billion to transfer to the Treasury account at the Fed, the required reserves of banks are freed up, and the money supply and reserves return to their prior levels.

If *banks* then buy the $10 billion of Treasuries from the market, deposits of the sellers increase by $10 billion, and banks transfer $200 million from excess reserves to required reserves at the Fed. The banking system has created $10 billion of new money supply: as banks buy Treasuries from investors, they create money in the accounts of the sellers, similar to the process of creating money when they make loans, and move a small amount of their excess reserves at the Fed to their required reserve accounts.

If *banks* buy all the $10 billion issue directly from the Treasury, then that amount is transferred from the Fed accounts of banks to the account of the Treasury. Deposits are still $10 billion above the starting point, and the banks' excess reserves are down by $200 million from the original level, as they were just after the Treasury disbursed the $10 billion from its Fed account.

So, when *banks* buy Treasuries, directly or from the market, the money supply (total deposits) increases, and the banks move a small percentage of their excess reserves at the Fed to their required reserve accounts.

In either case of banks investing in Treasuries, it takes only about $2 of their excess reserves to buy $100 of Treasuries. Since U.S. banks in total now have about $1.4 trillion of excess reserves, they could buy very large amounts of Treasuries.

D. Illustration of effects of open market operations or QE with Treasuries on aggregate portfolio of investments (referred from Chapter 2)

QE does not change the total amount of financial assets in the system, and does not change the mix of equities or international risk assets.

Suppose the Fed buys $2 of Treasury securities from the market: $1 relatively short-term & $1 bonds.

Then (aside from other market changes, such as stock volatility):

Aggregate balances for USD portfolio managers, investors, savers:

	Before QE $	After QE $
U.S. Stocks	250	250
U.S. Corporate and other bonds	150	150
Alternative Investments	100	100
Real Estate	100	100
International investments	100	100
"Cash and equivalents"	300	300
Bank checking and savings deposits	100	102
Bank time deposits	50	50
Treasuries –short-term	100	99
Treasury bonds	50	49
Total portfolio	**1000**	**1000**

So, in this illustration, the amount of Treasuries held by investors is reduced by the Fed, which provides bank deposits in exchange. The overall portfolio now has slightly more bank credit risk, since the proportion of bank deposits relative to Treasuries has increased. There is no other change in the credit risk or equity risk profile of the aggregate portfolio. And there is no fundamental reason for investors to now choose more international investments or other risk assets.

If the Fed buys other securities, in addition to Treasuries, then the total of financial assets still should not change, but the "other" bond portfolio declines some. Note that while investors trade with each other, there is no way for actions of investors to change the totals of deposits and Treasuries outstanding in aggregate. Changes in market prices can affect the total market values of stocks, bonds, and other assets. Since the total financial assets in the U.S. are about $150 trillion, if the Fed buys $1 trillion of securities, that amounts to less than 1% of the total.

E. Trust fund accounts (referred from Chapter 4)

The government has set up trust fund accounting for a number of different programs, including those related to Social Security, Medicare, highways, and railways. This appendix will focus on the Social Security trust fund as an example. The main point for purposes of this book is that these trust funds really represent accounting methods of keeping track of certain future obligations of the government, but do not involve the issuance of Treasury securities to the public and do not hold any securities that can be sold in the market.

Taxes received by the Treasury come from many sources: personal income tax, corporate, Social Security, tariffs, etc., and all go into what is essentially a big cash pot. That cash, plus cash raised from issuance of Treasury securities, is then used to make all kinds of payments: defense, housing, Social Security, Medicare, highways, etc. The arm of the government called the Social Security Administration has an arrangement to receive cash as needed from the Treasury, as do other departments of the government. The Social Security payments of the future will be made from normal Treasury cash flow, which will continue to come from the full array of taxes, supplemented when the Treasury issues net new notes to raise additional cash.

The Treasury also makes a bookkeeping entry, according to a formula, reflecting the legal requirements of Social Security legislation. The trust fund accounts provide a way to view actuarial estimations of future cash requirements for payments. But the trust has no real assets; in order for the payments to be made, the government will have to raise actual money at the time it needs it, through a combination of total tax revenue and issuance of tradable Treasury securities to the public. The SSA publishes year by year estimates of the extent to which Social Security taxes will support the payments, or need supplement from general funds. Those figures are much more useful than the trust fund estimates.

The trust fund concept is used, for historical reasons, as one way to view particular future obligations of the government, but certainly not all. The government has the obligation to pay for future years of military expenses, too, and many years of employee payrolls, and the future costs of congress, etc., but it would not be meaningful to record artificial funds today to represent the total of those future payments for many years.

The payments to be made by the government for each program are determined by law, not by the amounts recorded in the trust funds, and concerns about trust funds "running out of money" do not make sense. In fact, it would be easy to increase the size of any of the funds if we wanted to; it just wouldn't accomplish anything useful. Congress and the President could simply pass a law calling for an accounting entry adding to a trust fund account: it could be for $500 billion or $1 trillion dollars, or any other amount, at any time. That would just be a larger version of what is done each year: an accounting entry determined by law is added to the fund accounting balance each year.

Another example is sometimes helpful: Suppose that I set up a trust fund for my own future use during retirement. Then I spent all my money every year, saving none. But I filled the trust with promissory notes from myself – notes that said that I owed money to my own fund. The trust could have legal documentation, and could technically record millions of dollars, but it would all be meaningless. At my retirement, despite all the accounts of the trust fund, there would be no real money in it. It would simply be an accounting of IOU's from my right hand to my left. The question of whether I had enough in the account would be silly. The government trust funds contain only IOU's from the government. The question of whether the government has enough IOU's to itself cannot be meaningful.

For all these reasons, it does not make economic or financial sense to include such trust fund accounts in the computation of "national debt." That is why, for many years, the Treasury has been keeping track of Treasury securities "held by the public," which are much more meaningful figures.

About the Author

Frank Newman has had a very unusual career, including 30 years as a banking executive, in both the U.S. and China, and as the number two official of the U.S. Treasury Department.

He recently completed five years as Chairman of the Board and CEO of Shenzhen Development Bank, China. Mr. Newman led a team that turned the bank around substantially.

Previously, Mr. Newman served as Chairman and CEO of Bankers Trust, a major international bank based in New York.

In the 1990's, Mr. Newman served as Undersecretary, then Deputy Secretary of the U.S. Treasury. As the number two official of the Department, he represented it on a broad range of issues domestically and internationally, including economic and banking policy. He was awarded the Alexander Hamilton Award, the Department's highest honor.

Prior to government service, Mr. Newman served as Vice Chairman of the Board and Chief Financial Officer of BankAmerica Corporation, and Executive Vice President and CFO of Wells Fargo Bank.

Mr. Newman graduated from Harvard University with a BA, magna cum laude in economics.